BLACK BOY

NOTES

including
- *Life and Introduction*
- *List of Characters*
- *Critical Commentaries*
- *Character Analyses*
- *Critical Notes*
- *Review Questions*
- *Selected Bibliography*

by
Carl Senna, M.F.A.
Visiting Scholar, Brown University

INCORPORATED
LINCOLN, NEBRASKA 68501

Editor

Gary Carey, M.A.
University of Colorado

Consulting Editor

James L. Roberts, Ph.D.
Department of English
University of Nebraska

ISBN 0-8220-0242-6
© Copyright 1971
by
Cliffs Notes, Inc.
All Rights Reserved
Printed in U.S.A.

1998 Printing

Cliffs Notes, Inc.   Lincoln, Nebraska

CONTENTS

Black Boy Notes

LIFE OF THE AUTHOR

Richard Wright was born in 1908 on a plantation near Natchez, Mississippi. His father was a black sharecropper; his mother, a school teacher. In 1914, when cotton prices collapsed at the outbreak of the war, Wright's father was one among thousands who traveled North to the industrial centers; he got as far as Memphis where he found work as a night porter in a drugstore. The pressures of city living led him to desert his family shortly thereafter, and from then on Wright's childhood consisted of moving from one southern town to another, of intermittent schooling and sporadic jobs.

He arrived in Chicago during the Great Depression, worked at odd jobs and drifted until his association with the American Communist party gave him roots of a kind. Since the age of twelve Richard Wright had not only dreamed of writing, but had written. He was particularly attracted to the American naturalists — Mencken, Dreiser, Lewis, and Anderson — and his first publications included articles, short stories, and poetry, mostly printed by the Communist party press.

In 1938, his first book, *Uncle Tom's Children*, was published. These stories depict the Negro in revolt against his environment and they reveal the depth of Wright's emotional ties to the South. Each of the stories, in its violence and moral passion, is a preparation for his major publication, *Native Son*, in 1940. With this book Wright gained national attention, especially after it won the $500 prize awarded by *Story* magazine.

According to Wright himself, he was a member of the Communist party from 1932 to 1944, and the books he wrote during this period reflect his belief in communism as the only existing agency capable of restoring humanitarian values to the earth.

Native Son, incorporating this idea, influenced a whole generation of Negro novelists. The novel's anti-hero, Bigger Thomas, became the murderer he was, not out of choice, but as a result of environmental influences beyond his control; Wright's autobiography, *Black Boy* (1945), expresses the same Marxist philosophy. A best seller and a Book-of-the-Month Club selection, *Native Son* was successfully dramatized by Orson Welles and was made into a movie, Wright himself playing Bigger Thomas. The book is an integral part of American literary tradition in its struggle to reconcile the innocence of the rural past with the corruption of the urban present. Dreiser's *An American Tragedy* contains many of the same ideas and even a similarity of theme. Both Wright and Dreiser viewed society as the guilty instigator of criminality.

Yet naturalism as a literary form was not restricted to America. Throughout Western civilization in the nineteenth century, many writers were attempting to present life in all its detail, free of any preconceived notions of its meaning. Naturalism, closely akin to realism, presented a deterministic view of the universe. The writer's personality was kept in the far distance; the facts he exposed were meant to speak for themselves. Naturalism was, by its very nature, a form of social protest, and the Negro novelists who made up the so-called Wright School of Literature for the most part dealt with protest. There was Chester Himes' *If He Hollers Let Him Go* (1945), Ann Petry's *The Street* (1946), and Willard Savoy's *Alien Land* (1949); others included Carl Offord's *The White Face* (1943) and Lloyd Brown's *Iron City* (1951). The Wright School lasted past World War II. All this time Wright himself was undergoing important changes.

Wright's break with the Communist party involved a slow process of disillusionment. He discovered that even as a cell member, he was just as isolated, just as abused and misunderstood as he had been before. He finally resigned from the John Reed Club so that he could devote more time to writing and less to political action. Subsequently he was director of the Federal Negro Theater and a member of the Federal Writers' Project. Also, it was about this time that Wright became attracted to the existentialist philosophies of Sartre and, especially, Camus. He became an expatriate in 1947, living in France until his death. Although married, with two daughters, he always felt himself to be rootless, a wanderer. In 1953 he published *The Outsider,* in which the hero, Cross Damon, unlike Bigger Thomas, does not even attempt to become part of Western middle-class society. He turns his back on it completely. He ridicules Communist techniques and lives according to the existentialist principle of free choice. Cross Damon commits murder in a completely different spirit than Bigger Thomas. He acts as an individual who is free to do whatever his habits and desires lead him to do. He is not a victim of social and environmental pressures outside his control. In many ways Cross Damon, the outsider, resembles Meursault, the hero of Camus' *The Stranger.* Both men live outside of any involvement with common humanity and pay no attention to social mores.

After *The Outsider,* Wright wrote two novels, *The Long Dream* (1958) and *Lawd Today* (1963), both of which are concerned with race problems. He also wrote short stories, sociological studies, haiku, and numerous essays and reviews. His influence on current black writing is still powerful. He fathered one tradition — the Negro protest novel — and helped establish a new one: an exploration of naturalism using the American Negro as his subject. *Black Boy* is perhaps his most poignant and artistically successful book. In it, the ethics of living in the Jim Crow South are analyzed to their limits; he exposes all the unresolved issues that still haunt black and white Americans. Wright died abroad in 1960.

INTRODUCTION

Black Boy marks the culmination of Richard Wright's best-known period, his so-called Marxist period. As such, it must be treated separately from the books that followed. Although it is possible that he might have written this autobiography of his childhood the same way many years later, it is likely that his point of view would have been altered by the changes in his political philosophy. As it stands, *Black Boy* is as profoundly American as it is a distinctly Negro chronicle.

Written while Wright was a fervent Communist, the book explores the theory of human behavior determined by environment. Yet, innate in its fatalism is the author-narrator's ultimate escape from a rigid set of rules for survival. In Wright's boyhood, there was virtually no chance for a personality such as his to develop freely. Everything conspired against personal freedom— not only the white social structure, but the black as well. He was treated brutally and tyrannically at home in order to prevent his being treated the same way—or worse—outside the home. His parents, aunts, uncles, and grandparents enforced the code of conduct given to them by the white power structure: black children must never strive to be more than black children; if they do, not only will they suffer a terrible fate, but their families will as well. This way of life leads to a kind of society which has been called "pre-individualistic."

Pre-individualistic behavior is forced on one group of people by another. In this case, white southerners separated groups of people according to race. The result was that the individuals in the oppressed group became invisible; all that was left was a mass of faceless people. Yet the effects of this divisiveness are not limited to the oppressors. Within the oppressed community, individualism is considered dangerous; from the earliest age, a child is trained to behave according to the oppressor's view. If he does not obey, he will not be the only one to suffer the consequences. His whole community will be in danger. This pre-individualistic state existed particularly among Negroes only recently released from slavery. Although its primary effect was negative, its positive value was that it allowed black people to survive as a unit, with unusually close ties to one another. The migration into the urban centers and the North, however, destroyed this positive effect since to some Negroes the repressive quality of life at home was intolerable.

Richard Wright could not, from his earliest years, tolerate this repression, and *Black Boy* is the chronicle of his alienation, not only from white society, but from his own people. His protest springs from what the Spanish writer Unamuno calls "the tragic sense of life"; that is, it is more than a record of personal abuses. In *Black Boy* the protest is both personal and metaphysical—a cry of anguish in the face of the human condition. Tragedy is what comes of an individual's efforts to overcome the human condition. This is the spirit in which *Black Boy* was written—out of a sense of tragedy—yet it does not stop there.

What gives the book its unique place in American literature is its tone, as opposed to its content or structure. Its tone is that of the Blues. Lyrical and ironic, it is the song that follows the reality of pure tragedy. It accepts all that has happened and creates art from the pain of suffering. Ralph Ellison has written that "as a form, the Blues is an autobiographical chronicle of personal catastrophe expressed lyrically." There could be no better way to describe *Black Boy* and its unique voice in American letters.

LIST OF CHARACTERS

Richard Wright

The author-narrator, the "black boy" of the title.

Ella Wright

Richard's mother, whose illness prevents her from caring for herself and her children.

Nathaniel Wright

Richard's father, a victim of the Great Migration, who leaves his family early in Richard's life.

Alan Wright

Richard's brother; for most of their life he lives in Detroit with Aunt Maggie.

Grandpa

Ella's father, a disabled veteran of the Union Army.

Granny

Ella's mother, a Seventh-Day Adventist with whom Richard and Ella spend most of his childhood.

Aunt Addie

Ella Wright's sister; she is Richard's teacher in a religious school; at home, she is Richard's archenemy.

Aunt Maggie

A favorite of Richard's because of her sympathy and independence.

Uncle Hoskins

Aunt Maggie's husband, who is killed by whites.

Professor Matthews

Her second husband, who is chased from town by whites and always remains a mystery.

Uncle Clark

A cold and childless man who takes Richard to live with him in Greenwood.

Aunt Jody

Uncle Clark's wife, whose strict character repels Richard.

Uncle Thomas

A representative of all that Richard finds weak and hypocritical in black men.

Miss Simon

The head of the orphanage which Richard attends briefly. She tries and fails to win his trust.

Griggs

A classmate of Richard's whose attitudes are representative of many black boys he meets.

Reynolds and Pease

Two white racist co-workers.

Mr. Crane

A white Yankee employer of Richard's who advises him to go North.

Mrs. Moss

Richard's landlady, a warm but suffocating woman.

Bess

Her daughter who wants Richard to marry her.

Shorty

An elevator operator and friend of Richard's who sells himself daily to get a few pennies from whites.

Mr. Olin

The foreman in the optical house who sets up a fight between Richard and Harrison.

Harrison

A Negro employee of a rival optical house, he is used as a pawn in the fight with Richard.

Mr. Falk

An Irish Catholic co-worker of Richard's who helps him get books from the library.

CRITICAL COMMENTARIES

CHAPTER 1

The first chapter of the book establishes its theme and conflicts. It is not necessary to search for symbolic meanings. Each incident describes, in close detail, the emotions of the narrator. It is enough to be sensitive to his emotions and to the situations from which they spring. Since he is just a small child when these events occur, he is unconscious of their effect on his later manhood. However, the voice of the author — no matter how objective — provides order to what is otherwise chaos.

In the very first words of the book, Richard Wright establishes his distance from the four-year-old boy who sits in his grandmother's house in Mississippi. His grandmother is sick, and he has been warned several times by his mother to keep quiet; however, his rebellious personality is immediately revealed in the dramatic gesture of setting the house on fire. The reader then is immediately conscious of the nature of the narrator — not only by the scene he describes, but by his tone, which is objective and cool. It is clear that the child he was then is no stranger to him now. The writing serves as a telescope: it is the medium by which the past is clarified.

The punishment by his mother doesn't surprise the boy, except in its degree. She has almost killed him, and in his unconscious state he hallucinates about the udders of great white cows hanging over his head. He is terrified that they will drench him in some terrible liquid — surely a psychological reaction to his mother's ruthless beating, an aversion to life itself, her milk.

As the very first scene of the book, this episode establishes Richard's position as a rebel within his family; after surviving this beating, no amount of punishment can break his spirit. It is as if his mother's punishment has the reverse of the desired effect. By going to the limits of brutality with him at such a young age, she has released in him the power to survive beyond the normal bounds of human endurance.

Right off, it must be made clear that the complexity of the pre-individualistic society is such that love and hostility go hand in hand, as do cruelty and kindness, reward and punishment. Richard never questions his mother's love for him, and although he rarely mentions demonstrations of affection and although he stresses the negative aspects of his family life, the love between him and his mother is taken for granted. The perversion of this love — as an effect of slavery and oppression — is what upsets him and serves as the theme of the book.

The family's move to Memphis causes horrifying effects on the entire family. Richard's father becomes alienated and violent and, taking one of his father's careless commands at face value, Richard cruelly kills a kitten. Afterward he is horrified by what he has done, and his horror is underscored by his mother's religious, superstitious nature. She warns him of the dire consequences of taking a life and fills him with a sense of sin and guilt that will never leave him.

In these events lie clues to Richard's reactions to other events later on. For instance, although he is unconscious of the lifetime effect which his father's behavior will have on his psyche, in this one act — killing the kitten — Richard is responding to that effect. His father's place is restricted. He is a rural black, a man who has been uprooted and transplanted into an urban setting, completely out of his element. His bad temper and impatience is directly related to his personal frustrations, and Richard reacts to him likewise. If his father can't be decent, then Richard will be worse and, in that way, prove his own powers of aggression.

This becomes the model for Richard's relationships with other men thoughout the book. He will have no patience with their cowardice and will not fear humiliating them with his own masculinity. He is disgusted by males who allow themselves to be castrated by white society. His father is by no means the only one.

His mother's method of punishing him—with God and a beating—are also clues to Richard's later behavior. The God she chastises him with is a merciless oppressor—a kind of supernatural manifestation of white society. He has strict codes of conduct, demands instant obedience and, when defied, gives instant punishment. Richard's mother, here and elsewhere, uses God as another, more awesome term for white people in order to impress on her son the necessity to "stay in his place." God becomes many things; to whatever Richard's mother is unable to cope with or explain in human terms, He is introduced as the solution.

Under the circumstances, God is bound to fail very quickly. He is supposed to provide food when they are hungry, but He doesn't. Instead, it is clear to the boy that his father—and later his mother—is the breadwinner, not God. The whole question of food is not dropped there. When a preacher comes to dinner and greedily consumes the food Richard is longing for, he is, as God's representative, only increasing Richard's loss of faith. His hunger will remain throughout the book as a reality in itself and also as a cause for his alienation.

Richard begins to feel a constant hunger, soon associated with the disappearance of his father, who has deserted the family. Richard's mother goes to work, and he is forced to learn to make it on his own in the streets of Memphis. When he discovers that he can give as much violence as he has taken, he is free to go where he wants.

At six years old, Richard has no consciousness of racial differences: people are people. His grandmother can be termed white only because that is her natural color. And so the distinctions remain invisible to him. Life in the streets leads him to become a drunkard, hanging around a saloon and begging pennies from pedestrians. His mother beats him, prays for his salvation, and finally puts him in the care of an old woman. It is during this time that he develops a new kind of hunger—the hunger for knowledge—and with it comes his awareness of whites as separate from blacks.

Again, in each of these events are hints of larger revelations to come, especially as his consciousness develops. His mother's influence on him is naturally strong. The way she forces him to become independent, even tough, is something he finally appreciates. Above all, Richard wants to be a man. In the streets, in the saloon, in his explorations of the city, he exerts his masculinity, always unconsciously aware of the imminent castration of black boys and men. Yet, at the same time, he is developing a fascination with words—the secrets of the drunks—that will increase throughout his boyhood.

The frustration of his curiosity is described with the same cool fatalism as the other humiliations he endures. It comes from every direction—from his mother, as well as from white people—and whatever he tries to understand as information or moral truth results in only deeper misunderstanding. The world he occupies can only be described as hostile. And Richard begins to return this hostility with hostility. Sometimes it takes the form of shyness. When asked to perform in school, or to accept the attention of Miss Simon at the orphanage, he turns cold and cannot respond. He has learned to be suspicious of other people and there is a real danger that this suspicion will make him like the other members of his family—that is, incapable of giving and responding to love. Only by being conscious of the terrible consequences of such suspicion can he free himself as a man.

When he witnesses his father bowing and scraping, being an Uncle Tom before a white judge in order to avoid feeding his family, he can see clearly what he himself might become. It is a repulsive image to him, as is the image of his father, laughing with his new woman, all sensuality and no love. Later, he can excuse his father for this; he will be able to see him as an environmental prisoner. Now, however, as a boy, Richard has no tolerance for such a man.

In the conclusion of this chapter is a summary of Wright's philosophy on environment and man. It is a vision of society that encompasses the whole book, his whole childhood, and the people in it. Through his father's life he witnesses history and the present—the continuing effects of slavery on the children of slaves and their children too. The humiliated, disrupted lives of blacks under slavery did not end with emancipation. Although the people endured, they did so without the benefits of a civilized society. Civilization was left in Africa. All the traditions, habits, laws, and loyalties of a civilized society were removed from black people when they arrived as slaves in the New World. They were forced to live at the most elemental level. And Richard's father represents to him the effects of history—slavery—on the individual. Later he will forgive his father for neglecting his family, but it will not be a Christian forgiving; rather, it will be because of historical, Marxist reasons. This Marxist attitude is fundamental to the entire book and forms the basis for the Wright School of Literature. Naturalism is the aesthetic form the attitude takes because it excludes any preconceived ideas of morality. The narrator simply presents the facts, as history simply presents the facts, and they must speak for themselves.

CHAPTER 2

Although Chapter 1 establishes the conflicts basic to the book as a whole, it does so primarily in terms of Richard's immediate environment. His mother's efforts to make him comply with the standards set by a pre-individualistic society succeed only insofar as Richard can take care of himself. They fail, however, in keeping him unconscious of his own individuality. He is ready to measure his condition against others, and Chapter 2 demonstrates his growing awareness of a world outside his own.

His mother tries to protect him from seeing his condition for what it is. She wards off his questions about white people and succeeds in keeping their reality remote. But the results of this protection are to make white people fantastic and unreal in his imagination; even his relationship to other Negroes is unrealistic. In two separate incidents, he sees Negroes in uniform—as soldiers and prisoners—and he is terrified by the reality of the nightmare. They seem more like *animals* than people, and he wants to understand *why* they are what they are. His mother evades him, but lets him know vaguely that white people are somehow responsible. She does not tell her son about white oppression and crushed black dignity, yet his innocent eyes see the truth: slavery in its rawest form—the slaves themselves. Thus the attempts to keep Richard ignorant continue to have the opposite of the desired effects. The murder of Uncle Hoskins, the silence about the white world, and religious explanations for natural events only serve to fire his imagination.

It is easy to see how Richard develops an aversion to Christianity which lasts throughout his life. An awareness of guilt and sin is brutally imposed on him by his grandmother. Even his mother finally finds the atmosphere at the grandmother's too oppressive for them. Richard's greatest sin is his curiosity, and every opportunity his imagination has to expand is promptly squelched. His grandmother, for instance, beats him for a foul-mouthed remark he utters in complete innocence; his difficult relationship with her will play a large part in his development. To Granny, any deviation from her concept of the norm is subjected to the most severe punishment. The hypocrisy of these hard judgments, couched in Christian ideology, does not escape the boy, and he will not forget them as a man.

A recurrent response to his condition throughout the book is a series of pastoral contacts with nature. Nature serves as a balm to his injuries and, in relation to the seasons and natural wonders, he is able to express his emotions freely. This is one of the more striking American qualities about the book—reminiscent of Thomas Wolfe, Walt Whitman, Sherwood Anderson, and many others.

Just as Wright can understand his father as "a creature of the earth" who is bewildered and finally driven away from the city, so have hosts of other American writers been obsessed with the vision of an innocent, pastoral, lost world. It is a world they strive to recapture, while doubting its existence. Though none of them would deny that "violence is as American as cherry pie," there is some mysterious conviction within much American writing that there is the possibility of a pure soul and a humane personality. Nature is the medium through which these writers try to symbolize this pure state — be it the nature of earth or the nature of man. The most lyrical passages in *Black Boy* are invariably concerned with Richard's love of the natural world, and they stand apart — both in content and style — from the rest of the book, like a lovely, lonely Blues song.

Richard's relationship to the natural world is direct and simple. Outdoors, among the trees and birds, a boy can express his emotions freely. Although he is conscious of the good *and* the evil forces at work in the open air, he feels his individual self expand and develop naturally. He is not judged or repressed. He is just alive. For some people, it is possible to feel more at home in a tree or an empty field than indoors, among his own people. For Richard, as a boy, this is the case and throughout the book he will return to the natural world to find metaphors for freedom and joy.

Richard is so eager to learn and so consistently suppressed, it is incredible to see how resilient the imagination can be. He won't stop asking questions, and if he gets no answers, his imagination takes over, providing what reality conceals. In this chapter we see him becoming aware of his condition in symbolic terms. He is affected emotionally by the things that happen to him; but, without answers to his questions about these events, they are only symbols.

The more he grows and travels, the more he becomes conscious of race. The murder of one uncle and the threat of death to another by whites — both of these intensify the fear that has been growing in him slowly but surely. As this fear increases —

for the enemy is real—Richard becomes superstitious. He has lists of antidotes to real and unreal dangers. Unable to perform when called upon—shy, but still rebellious—his imagination plays a larger and larger role in his life. It is his escape hatch into a better world or into oblivion; it is also the armor he wears against the wounds inflicted by the society he lives in.

CHAPTER 3

The workings of a child's mind are often confused in retrospect. The combination of his awakening senses, his parents' authority, and the world of his contemporaries make it nearly impossible to discover the individual in the child. Wright's objective voice helps to clarify these confusing elements to himself and to the reader. Conscious of Freud's observations about human behavior and steeped in the writers of his time—including James Joyce—Richard Wright is, in a sense, analyzing himself as he writes the book. This self-analysis persists chapter by chapter, and very soon the individual boy begins to emerge as more than a so-called rebel without a cause. He begins to understand what has been troubling him and why, and this leads him to make distinctions between just and unjust rage.

As with most people, the first and most fundamental test of who he is as an individual comes among his contemporaries. There he develops a personality, unique and separate, as a member of a larger social order. First we see Richard among his friends where he plays out traditional boyhood roles, ranging from joker to tough guy. Yet in this section, Wright is not simply reproducing the standard games children play. He is showing how a particular culture is preserved and how a tradition is maintained by the offspring. The boys' attitudes toward themselves and toward white people are the attitudes they have been given by their parents. Richard is no misfit among them. They are all young and curious and full of their masculinity. An awareness of the white world, however, hangs ominously over all their words, and soon enough they are prisoners of their society, engaged in warfare with white boys. It is a one-way street. Before these boys have time to let their imaginations plan what they will do as men, they are trapped in a historical role. This is what lack of opportunity means. Blacks cannot hope like whites can. Blacks exist only in order to set themselves up against white people. Their value as a people is determined by whites. For a time it looks as if Richard will fit right into this pattern. All the factors in his life have been arranged so that he will.

But all of this is shattered, his life disrupted again, by his mother's stroke and paralysis. He goes with her to Granny's where she is tended by her brothers and sisters. They respond to her illness in a way that demonstrates other qualities that emerge from the society Richard inhabits. Out of the devastation and terror of their lives, not only have his people learned to endure oppression or use it against one another; they have also learned to support each other in times of trouble. They live as one body, sometimes inflicting wounds on itself; but, just as often, giving another member the will to survive.

Richard's attachment to his mother is foremost in his life. When she becomes ill, Richard goes to Greenwood with Uncle Clark and Aunt Jody because Greenwood is close to his mother. However, his stay with them is a miserable failure. His aunt and uncle mean well, but he cannot adjust to their attitudes toward him. Obsessed by a fear of death, always worried about his mother, he finally begs to be sent back to Granny's, thus disrupting his schooling again.

Richard hates being in his grandmother's house, but his one link with other people – his mother – is there. His mother, trapped within her sickness as they all are trapped within their environment, has once again unknowingly contributed to his independence. It is through her sickness that Richard is changed from a rebel without a cause into an individual with a fixed attitude toward life. This attitude will remain with him throughout his life. It comes from being a witness to the helpless suffering of the person he loves most in the world. His mother's paralysis, in his own words, grows into a symbol in his mind – a symbol of the years that have come before and will come after. The futile wandering, the useless effort, the oppression and insecurity of their lives — and all life — is going to haunt him until his own death. Because of his view of the world, he will never be able to participate fully in happiness, and he will feel at home only with others who share his attitude.

CHAPTER 4

The American artist has been called an Ishmael, doomed to wander on the outskirts of his society. Misunderstood or ignored by those with whom he longs to communicate, this Ishmael often ends up in exile from his people or in desolation among them. When young Richard Wright comes to view those he loves most with the eyes of an outsider, he is for a time unaware of his membership among the American Ishmaels.

In this chapter we see the origins of an artistic temperament as it develops under extraordinary conditions. At home with Granny, Richard is subjected to severe religious discipline. She is a woman who is completely antilife. All the pleasures of the senses are condemned as sinful; even the food she serves is drained of any taste. Her youngest daughter, Addie, is a carbon copy of Granny, and she and Richard engage in vicious battles. He sees normal boys reduced to docile pupils by the religious education Aunt Addie provides. Worse yet, the boys have none of the moral fiber Richard has found in street gangs. In one incident a fellow student is too obedient to admit his guilt for a certain act and lets Richard take the blame.

However, this is only one feature of Richard's religious life. It is perhaps the strongest, but there is a subtle side to religion which Richard doesn't miss. It is the artistic element that catches his imagination and nourishes his interest in language. There is beauty in the hymns and mystery in the ritual. Religion gives order where there was only chaos and it provides many metaphors for human existence and suffering. Richard's recurrent exposure to these elements affects him deeply. The poetry of the words and songs moves his senses and his mind. It will ultimately give him the passion to write his own poetry.

There is, also, another way in which religion influences Richard. Because it is based on an ideology which, in its ideal form, cuts across boundaries set by race and nation, Christianity frees the young boy from his blackness. The possibilities of a brotherhood based on common ideals are latent in religion and, to one who is sensitive to these ideals, it is liberating. Therefore, through his purest religious experience, Richard is freed both as an artist and a man. However, this only makes the hypocrisy of his home life all the more intolerable to him and accounts for his ability to separate God from religion. He does not believe in God, but he is moved by a religious instinct. He cannot pretend to follow Granny in her Seventh-Day Adventist fanaticism, but he cannot stop himself from having strong moral feelings. One of the novel's most sensitive scenes focuses on this point. There is a misunderstanding—by now common—between himself and Granny and it results in her humiliation in church. Richard is truly apologetic and promises to pray for salvation. It is in the process of this prayer, when he finds nothing to say to God, that he conceives his first story. It is thrilling to him, and now writing begins to enter his life as a great release and joy. The isolation and concentration required of him give his imagination a chance to soar. His spirit is liberated, and he is able to transform the sorrows of being an outsider into the strengths of writing down his feelings. He shows the story to a girl he knows and her bewilderment at its existence, as opposed to its meaning, gives him real pleasure.

Finally, Richard is given up as a lost cause by his family; they expect nothing of him anymore, so he is free to do as he chooses. This marks a change in his character. No longer one who struggles against his family in order to win their approval, he turns his rebellion outside—to the world at large. We see, therefore, in this chapter how Wright is becoming everything his environment has intended him not to be. As an outsider, an Ishmael, a masculine individual, and a believer in human rights, he is dangerous to his community. Just why he is dangerous, and how, becomes increasingly clear as he matures.

CHAPTER 5

The freedom that Richard has achieved by the age of twelve is unusual. It is a freedom of many facets. He no longer receives orders from Granny and Addie; they have given up on him. At the same time, this freedom from their criticism is also a freedom from their interest in him, and is perhaps an example of how the lack of tenderness he sees between black people actually evolves. But, if Addie and Granny have no concern for Richard, he too is free of any concern for them. The unspoken pact between them means that they will no longer care about each other. And for one who is already an outsider, it is a relief not to be forced to show affection or demonstrate loyalty. This is, in itself, a form of freedom.

Since most children are rebellious and individualistic, it can be assumed that this form of freedom was achieved by many other black boys besides Richard. What slavery and its aftermath of fear had done was to make parents and grandparents protect those children they could repress and reject those they couldn't. To this extent, Richard was probably typical. He was sent out into the world to fend for himself without much support at home.

At twelve years old, Richard has had only one full year of school, but when he reenters school, he is advanced to the sixth grade. Granny's reaction is to see Richard as more peculiar than ever. Here we see him relating to the outside world on its own terms. He is a complete individual—both intellectually curious and capable of waging physical warfare. His qualifications are fine for any gang, but his aspirations are destined to be squelched.

Richard's friends work on the weekends, but Granny forbids him to do so, which means he can't join his friends during lunch hour shopping sprees. Knowing that Granny won't let him out after he has gone home, he forfeits meals in order to explore his environment. He is learning what his priorities are now. By necessity he is educating himself, and this involves extensive choices, choices that are usually imposed by others.

One of the most crucial of these choices comes with his experience selling newspapers. The job is highly rewarding: it gives him a chance to earn money and a chance to read adventure stories in the supplement section of the paper. His imagination is on fire; he loves to read. But then comes the awful discovery that the newspaper's publishers are racist. Granny and Addie have been giving him many reasons for thinking himself wicked. He has rejected them all. With this discovery, he judges himself on his own terms. With all the benefits the job gives him, it is morally wrong for him to continue it.

In the summer he takes a job that he enjoys — as an assistant to an insurance salesman. They travel into the Delta country and to plantations where Richard measures himself against the poor, illiterate children there. They look up to him as one who is "city-fied," successful, and admirable. It's a new experience for him — to be treated as a model for others. And for once he gets plenty to eat. He wants to continue the job, but his employer dies — another in a series of letdowns.

With Richard's grandfather's death, we have a portrait of practically an invisible man in the house. It is as if he assumes substance in Richard's life only when he is dying. He takes on a historical rather than a personal significance, for he served in the Union Army and, disabled, spent the remainder of his life expecting the government to send him the pension he deserved. His brief life history sums up the history of black Americans. Any soldier is a slave. And a black soldier is a slave's slave. Once again Richard is conscious of whites as an abstract force of evil.

Outside of the writers whom Richard comes to admire, there are no male models in his life. His grandfather has remained all but invisible. Those men he has had contact with have repelled him. He hates their failure to rebel when they are the potential righters of wrong. The life of his grandfather only affirms the growing impression he has of blacks as unconscious co-conspirators in a racist system. In his later work, Wright seems to be saying that every act short of killing is an act of cowardice on the part of a black man. And perhaps if his grandfather had gone out and shot a white man in revenge for his tragic life, Richard would have had one male model to look up to. Instead, he witnesses one frustration after another and it all contributes to his growing rage.

Richard himself has learned to rebel. His mother trained him to defend himself in the streets by locking the door on him. In this chapter we see that the act of rebellion cannot be separated from one's life style. It is natural for Richard to resist his grandmother when her commands are irrational. It doesn't involve thought or planning. When he threatens to leave her house if she doesn't allow him to work, he means it. He is not playing on her sympathies. He is a rebel, and so Granny gives in. For this successful act of resistance, he receives a kiss from his mother who, with that one gesture, sums up the tragic losses of her own life.

CHAPTER 6

The ethics of living Jim Crow require that Richard be abject, obedient, and silent—a slave in everything but name. Yet everything we know about his character has prepared us to expect rebellion. He might be shy and reserved, but he is nobody's pawn. How he will, in fact, deal with the shock of confronting real white people is completely unpredictable. He craves the independence and the necessities which a job will provide. But how much of himself will he have to sell in order to buy those things?

His first confrontation is disastrous. His employer, a female, does more than abuse his race and his humanity. She abuses his aspirations — to be a writer — and he cannot return to work for her afterward. His next job at least brings him good food. But he is astounded by the way the white family treats one another. Richard is at first shocked, then curious, at their behavior. It makes for good stories at school, although he is exhausted by the work itself.

Oddly, it is not really through his relations with these people that we are exposed to his reactions toward whites. Rather, it is through his response to his Uncle Tom, who has moved in with them, that we see the intensity of his rebellious feelings about Jim Crow society. His refusal, on violent terms, to let his uncle beat him for speaking forthrightly, is his refusal to live by the standards of his time. He will not be anyone's slave or anyone's whipping boy. His uncle says that this rebellious spirit will lead him to the gallows, never considering that it might lead him far beyond the gallows. Richard can react only with contempt for his uncle, because he has learned, through his jobs, the significance of all the baffling beatings he has received at home. He sees how these beatings fit into the whole social structure and he refuses to participate.

CHAPTER 7

Aside from the book's aesthetic and historical value, *Black Boy* gives important insights into the evolution of a writer. The shocks and blows he has received so far could have happened to any number of black children at that time in the South. Why, then, did Richard Wright's character take an exceptional turn?

Ever since his mother's illness and the changes it brought to his life style, Richard has been increasingly unable to communicate and participate with his contemporaries. For a brief time it appears he might at least have the pleasure of friendship and companions in school. (If he had, perhaps he never would have left the South or written. Perhaps he would have been able to adjust his personality to the Jim Crow way of life, and he would have remained anonymous — one of many "black boys.") But his mother's illness has made a permanent difference in his nature, and this difference combined with the forces of rebellion and individualism to form Richard Wright the writer.

As he moves from job to job, from the seventh to the eighth grade in school, he is always conspicuous by his attitude of detachment. It makes him unpopular not only with his co-workers, but with his classmates. He has a short story printed in the local Negro newspaper, and most of the people he knows are completely bewildered by it. A black boy is not supposed to do those things.

The provincialism of his people is both a good and a bad thing in this case. While they upbraid and try to shame Richard, instead of embracing and praising him for his accomplishment, they are also unable to see the larger design in this small event. Therefore, there is no one who can warn him, in realistic terms, against trying to fulfill his dreams of being a writer. If there had been someone around with the sophistication to know the dangers and hazards in the path his life was taking, he might have been stopped. But there is no one to do that, and so he nurtures his dreams.

CHAPTER 8

Richard's dreams and his stories are an escape for him when he is fourteen and fifteen, but only a temporary escape. His work, his home, and his acquaintances create a circle of insecurity and sorrow around him. He can't escape them or their stories. He hears how Negroes are killed by whites for stepping out of line; people he knows receive that "reward" for the slightest slip. He must always be on guard against the same fate — or at least until he can get away from this repressive environment.

At fourteen, Richard has a view of life far beyond his years, but he also has the vulnerability of a child. As he sees himself increasingly ostracized by his friends and family, he is hurt more and more and he retreats deeper and deeper into himself. When he overhears his Uncle Tom warning his cousin to stay away from him because he is no good, his heart snaps inside of him. It is the final wound, and he knows that he must leave home as quickly as possible.

There is a special kind of tension that comes with being misunderstood. On the one hand, one is determined to prove society wrong and to show people who you really are. On the other hand, there is always a tendency to accept another person's judgment, and, in so doing, become the very person you are seen to be. On an individual level, this tension is building up in Richard day by day; on a racial level, he sees it happening to all Negroes in the South.

He has been told, at home, as long as he can remember, that he is worthless and bad. A part of him wants to live up to this reputation, even though it is false. Another part of him is constantly rebelling against that judgment. He sees the people around him accepting the white man's opinion on blackness. They are taking the easiest, and safest, course. He is disgusted by this, and his Uncle Tom represents what is most cowardly about his people.

At school the same problem arises. Given the honor of writing the valedictory address, Richard is shocked to discover that it is all a fraud. The principal has a prepared speech for him to read because there will be white people present in the audience. Richard refuses to read anything but his own speech, against everyone's advice. As a result, he is more ostracized than ever. Ironically, he is now considered to be even more evil, although he has responded to the part of himself which refuses to accept that judgment. It is 1925, and Richard is almost seventeen when he goes out to face the world.

CHAPTER 9

The world young Wright faces is, in many ways, similar to the one he has left behind. Home and school have prepared him, psychologically, for the shock of working with whites. He is a victim of their racist arrogance, just as he is also a victim of Granny's and Aunt Addie's terrible righteousness. The difference is in the response he is able to give.

He is beaten up by whites passing in a car; he is fired from one job for witnessing the beating of a black woman by whites; he is tortured by two white co-workers in an optical house — and in all these cases, he is not allowed to respond as a man. At least at home he could fight back or argue his side of the story and, even if it led nowhere, he had the small satisfaction of responding like a human being. But in the world he now occupies daily, he is stripped of his manhood. In order to survive, he has to bow and scrape before these white individuals. A look in his eyes, a silent declaration of self-esteem, is enough to have him kicked or fired. And he cannot control the look in his eyes. He is being humiliated daily and he can't even communicate his rage to a Negro friend, Griggs, who gets him the job in the optical house, where a Yankee is boss. Griggs tells him that when he's in front of white people, he must *think* before he acts, *think* before he speaks. Richard's way of doing things is all right among blacks, but is wrong for *white* people. They won't stand for it.

Richard knows that Griggs is right, that is, insofar as survival is the first concern of a man. And Richard wants to survive. But he also wants to go North, he wants to write, and he wants to be a man. Without these dreams for the future, he would become what his family has predicted: a two-bit criminal who will end up on the gallows. For the sake of the future, he puts his manhood aside and tries the new job.

His employer is sympathetic, but his co-workers are out to get him. And here Richard suffers the deepest humiliation yet. Tortured and bullied by the two whites, he leaves work, determined never to return. But Mr. Crane, the boss, calls him back and asks for an explanation. He cannot give it, for fear of the fate he will receive, and he comes close to breaking down. All he can say is that he's going North. The boss agrees and Richard leaves, ashamed of himself to the depths of his being. He has not even, in this case, been successful at Jim Crow living. He has not managed, like Griggs, to avoid the abuse of whites by pandering to their whims. Yet he has not managed, either, to respond like a man. He has only one thought: escape.

CHAPTER 10

Now that Richard is fully conscious of his limitations, he is just about ready to transform them into assets. If he can't be one thing, he will be another. He is desperate to leave Jackson, to start the slow journey to the North. But he has to have money to do so and he is consistently fired from one job after another because of the look in his eyes. At first his blackness is all that white people see, but then—to their shock—they notice a certain expression in his eyes and they are afraid of him. They don't want him around anymore because he won't play "nigger."

In his novels, Richard Wright explores in depth the evolution of a criminal. He sees criminality as arising inevitably from certain social strains. It is as inevitable as mixing certain ingredients to make a cherry pie. He views the individual as being without personal responsibility for his crime. The criminal's actions are beyond his own control. Social forces have conspired to produce them.

In his desperate state, Richard is given only one option for escape, and that is crime. Although he is, by training and temperament, too sensitive, sensible, and moral to make crime his business, he is, under the circumstances, prepared to take advantage of its existence. There is no other way out. He will have to steal the money for his escape.

He does not arrange the situation easily. It's a simple matter of graft, and he needs only two hundred dollars. But the mental agony he suffers is the price he pays for it. Later, he will be able to write about crime out of this experience; he will, in fact, be obsessed by it in most of his writing. But as he lives it, the risks are overwhelming, and he is fraught with fear.

It doesn't help that this is the single act in his life that his family would have expected of him. As such, it is the last thing he wants to do. But he does do it, because there is nothing else for him. He is successful and he gets what he wants in a short period of time. But instead of being tempted to continue the gamble, he stops at the limit he set for himself, packs his bags, promises his mother that he will send for her, and leaves Jackson for Memphis.

Richard learns that crime means suffering and he wants no part of it. More than that, it solves nothing in the way of social problems. It might, temporarily, soothe an individual's pain. But it does not contribute to a social revolution. Consistent with the point of view expressed so far, Wright responds to this experience on a social, rather than a moral, basis. He concludes that crime is only evil insofar as it fails to improve society. Criminality occurs when all other opportunities have been cut off; it serves a transitory need. Richard's suffering is foremost in this situation. And even though he is now liberated, he is neither happy nor hopeful. The future is as fearful as ever.

CHAPTER 11

Most autobiographical writing has two points of view: that of the writer as he was then and that of the writer as he exists in the present. Consequently many of the conclusions which Wright draws from his early behavior are seen only in retrospect; at the time about which he is writing he was unaware of many factors. Looking back, even seemingly blind actions have a significant motive. The writer learns who he was, and is, by writing. As we follow, step by step, the evolution of Richard Wright's personality, we must believe him more than we believe the narrator of a work of fiction. The objective quality of Wright's voice throughout *Black Boy* gives the tale an authority it might otherwise lack.

When he arrives in Memphis in 1925, Richard is on his own for the first time in his life. He is separated from his family, not only by miles but by money. He has no choice but to succeed. Yet, in spite of his many experiences as a young black in a tough world, he is still naive in many ways. We know this not because we are told, but because Wright shows us. His relationship, for example, with his landlady, Mrs. Moss, is such that the reader is as confused about her as Richard is. He is overwhelmed at once by her warmth and her tolerance—two characteristics he rarely found at home. He doesn't want to be suspicious of her, but he is. She offers him her house, her food, her friendship, and her daughter.

To Richard, this type of woman is completely new. Therefore he cannot go by any former experience in dealing with her daughter, Bess; he must follow his instincts, which tell him to refuse her. At all times the possibility of his being trapped in an irreversible situation is present. It's a new kind of danger—less violent and obvious than those he has encountered before—but nevertheless it is a danger.

Mrs. Moss is a universal type of woman, and once he has learned how to deal with her, he will know much more about women in general. She is a woman whose maternal and erotic instincts are at variance with each other; and, in order to relieve her frustrations at the restrictions of age and society, she must use her daughter as a vicarious means of obtaining erotic satisfaction for herself, while forming an ultra-maternal relationship with the lover in question. There is nothing either conscious or malicious about her responses to people. But her frustration makes her dangerous.

It takes a while for Richard to establish with Mrs. Moss and her daughter a relationship that is suitable for them all. But when he realizes that they are as innocent as he is, he is able to act like a man rather than an ignorant boy.

It is through an experience like this that the reader can see that Richard is approaching maturity. The writing is convincing not by being highly emotional, nor by being unrealistic in its conclusions; it is convincing because the boy is becoming the man who is writing the book, and the two points of view are beginning to merge into one voice.

CHAPTER 12

Because Memphis is a larger, more cosmopolitan city than Jackson, there are slight differences in social behavior which Richard quickly recognizes. He works in an optical company with about twelve whites — ranging from Ku Klux Klanners to several Jews and a Catholic — and several Negroes. The elevator operator, Shorty, a light-skinned Negro, comes to represent what Richard fears and dislikes most in the world. Shorty lets himself be kicked and abused by the whites in the building; he makes a big joke of it in order to pick up an extra tip. He makes a farce out of the relationship between blacks and whites, reducing it to comic sado-masochism.

Richard feels nothing but contempt for Shorty, who is able to let these things happen only because he has given up hope for change or escape. His intelligence and literacy don't matter to him. Although he hates white people, he will let them step all over him for the most trivial, monetary reward. Shorty is not the only one used by whites, however; Richard and another Negro boy, Harrison, who works for a rival optical house across the street, are soon used as pawns by whites. It is a grotesque situation in which they are made to mistrust each other in spite of their knowing, reasonably, there is nothing to fear. The whites, however, manipulate the two black boys' minds to the extent that they have no control over their emotions. It is only when Richard and Harrison are fully suspicious of one another that the whites reveal their motives. They want the two black boys to fight for five dollars while they watch. Richard resists the temptation for money many times but is finally persuaded by Harrison that they will only play at fighting, so he agrees.

The result is a disaster and a humiliation beyond Richard's wildest dreams. It is, in fact, one of the only experiences in the book where we are conscious of some reluctance on the part of the writer to reveal the experience. It is something from which he will never recover, not only for personal reasons, but because of the larger implications. He, like Shorty, has allowed himself to be "used" — for money.

Wright feels the effects of slavery still alive in himself, as they are alive in the whole society around him. He might as well be back on the plantation listening to his master's voice. Although the whites don't know who he is, they have structured the society against ever knowing him; as a result, he and they are inescapably bound together. His hatred for himself springs from his hatred for them. It seems that the only way Richard can redeem himself is by finding some measure of forgiveness for them.

CHAPTER 13

It has been said by Frank O'Connor, the Irish writer, that most writers have one thing in common: they both love and hate the place of their origins. Richard Wright certainly fits into this category; but it is only toward the end of his autobiography that the conflict in his feelings becomes clear. Up until now, the reader has picked up only distant strains of nostalgia and affection for the South. Love has been but a minor refrain throughout the book. Yet its presence is always felt and it accounts for the Blues-like quality of the book.

Now, in the thirteenth chapter, Richard enters into a state of mind which will bring both an attachment to, and a liberation from, the South. First, he happens to read an article about H. L. Mencken, and the very fact that Mencken is being attacked draws Richard toward him. He longs to read him, but it is only by the most circuitous method that he can achieve the simple satisfaction of getting into a library. A white co-worker, who is Catholic and therefore maligned by most southerners, lends Richard his library card. This is the beginning of his self-education.

Through Mencken's essays, Richard learns the names of other American writers, as well as learning how prose can be used as a weapon. This is all Richard needs. To discover that the pen can be as mighty as the sword is a terrific surprise to him; and then to read these other writers (who also feel themselves alienated from the American scene) is a revelation.

Through reading Dreiser, Sherwood Anderson, and the major European writers, Wright not only begins to understand himself better, but to understand white people too. They are no longer so strange and impenetrable to him. Yet he must conceal from everyone what he is learning. He continues to work and to read and to play dumb for the benefit of his own survival and in order to bring his mother and brother to Memphis. But he is undergoing the final stage in his painful growth, and his secret world is his most important world.

What should have been a joy, a liberation, and a means of communication, however, are for Richard just the opposite. He has no one with whom he can talk about his discoveries or his dreams. There is no guarantee that they will come to fruition. He considers the alternatives, however, to pursuing these dreams and they are so horrible that he ends up without a choice. He is coming to realize just how unalterable human character is. And although he is conscious of the many forces that have conspired to make him what he is, there still remains a mystery as to why he should be so profoundly alienated from ordinary people. He cannot change who he is or what course he must follow. Any other course would make him not only miserable, but he wouldn't even be successful pursuing it. Yet he cannot feel any relief in knowing who he is. To be both an American writer and an American black is to be permanently in exile, an outsider on one's own native soil. Richard has no choice now in being a writer, just as he has never had a choice in being the man or the color that he is.

CHAPTER 14

It is now only a matter of money and opportunity before Richard will go North. These problems are resolved because he has learned how to play the role which his family and white people expect of him. He can play it in spite of the tension and deception it involves, now that he sees a light at the end of the tunnel. His people are no more aware of his inner life than are the white folks he works with. And so, always isolated and secretive, he makes his escape under a completely false pretext.

The voice of the boy Richard and the man Richard Wright have now merged into one. In flight he feels no elation or promise, but only the tension and fear he has grown accustomed to living with. He is not going toward something so much as away from something else. His whole life so far has been one of upheaval, travel and flight, so this experience in itself is far from new to him.

Yet, as he moves, he is at least conscious of what the motive means. This is the difference, and the only one, between his journey now and all the ones that came before. He knows what it means to be leaving the South, to be American, to be black, to be a writer. He is nobody's victim, not even his own, as long as he can maintain this consciousness. It is the only freedom he knows and it began with that first overwhelming revelation he had at his mother's bedside: the "conviction that the meaning of living came only when one was struggling to wring a meaning out of meaningless suffering." Henry James has said that consciousness is the only thing left to a man in the end. And this is Wright's conclusion now; to be conscious of meaninglessness is preferable to faking a meaning—that is, it is the only possible state of mind for him.

The terrible price of this awareness is that Wright knows that he is what he is forever. And he will always be a southern product, perhaps transplanted in another climate, perhaps to blossom there away from home, but always southern. It is this past which he must struggle to understand and by understanding, forgive, as he lives in the North and elsewhere. He has some faith that this will happen and, when it does, he will at least feel that those people who have done everything in their power to destroy him, will, by his survival, have to change their ways. This is his revenge — to take the whole of himself, and so much of himself is the South, away; to do more than endure; to flourish as an individual.

He has won a victory over the cruelty of humanity just by leaving the place of his birth. By his voluntary release, he has proved the whole system to be a fraud and a failure. This might, for some men, be sufficient cause to rejoice. But it takes the wisdom of Richard Wright to find no pleasure in victory. Instead he maintains, to the very end, his austere and poetic response to the whole of mankind.

CHARACTER ANALYSES

RICHARD WRIGHT:

Because Richard is growing throughout the book, his character is always changing. The small child we see at the beginning is a far cry from the seventeen-year-old at the end; yet there is a fundamental core which remains the same. He is a rebel and, as such, an outsider, from the very beginning.

Through his descriptions of people's reactions to him, Wright gives us a sense of the impression he makes on others. He offends most everyone, not for overt acts of defiance against them, but because of the attitude he expresses. He has few friends, but has no real enemies. He is not aggressive, but his presence is threatening. Unable to participate naturally in fun and games, he is irritating to those who do. Almost no one likes to have him around.

What social forces conspired to make him into this type of individual is the question that Richard Wright, the narrator, is trying to solve as he writes. It is said that one's character is pretty much formed by the age of four and, afterward, it can only be modified to one degree or another by experience. Although Wright emphasizes social circumstances in creating an individual, he starts his autobiography with a solid characterization of himself as a child. There is, then, always a conflict between which is the stronger influence: character or society.

The question of how and why Wright's character was formed is hardest for him to answer in terms of his own development. It involves the complex problems of personal guilt as opposed to social guilt, personal responsibility as opposed to social responsibility. In the end, he can make no clear-cut distinctions between one or the other. Why he becomes who he is, or why he is the person he is becoming are two inseparable questions.

The reader is always conscious of the unique nature of the author. In many ways he seems to consider himself exempt from normal human fallacies. Ruthless in his condemnation of any weakness, he is rarely self-critical. What he ultimately discovers in his self-analysis is that his reactions have been justifiable. This quality of egotism gives the book a strident tone at times, which confirms what he is saying about himself; that is, Wright is not a sociable person, but a critical observer who alienates others by his moral position.

Given the circumstances of his life, Richard the boy and Wright the author do in fact hold a justifiable position. Viewed as coldly as it is in *Black Boy*, society is invariably and simply wrong. Richard is not a deviant personality, but a natural product of his circumstances. This is what the book is telling us. Richard Wright is not going to soothe anyone's nerves.

If, therefore, the reader finds the tone of the book irritating, it is inevitable. The questions Wright is raising can only have answers that are serious and upsetting. These are the questions Richard has been asking himself from a very early age: why is my family disrupted? Why is Granny oppressive? Why do my friends and I have such limited futures? Why do white people set out to destroy me? What have I done as an individual to deserve this treatment from society? And how can I escape? Richard has to come to terms with his own personal history by escaping from the place where it endures. And he has to conceive of his past and write about it as if it were typical, in order to understand and answer those questions. This is his legacy for the future of black and white America.

ELLA WRIGHT

It is difficult to get a clear impression of Richard's mother. This is one of the difficulties in writing about people close to one; one is unable to see them as types. It is often simpler to treat such people only in subjective terms; that is, how does *she* affect *me.*

Richard's mother is a solid presence throughout the book. She tongue-lashes him often, beats and slaps him, and seems to be very stern, a replica of her own mother. Yet somehow one senses that Richard may have received some of his training in rebellion from her. She is not happy living in the religious household they are forced so often to inhabit, and she even rewards Richard with a kiss when he successfully revolts against his grandmother's will. Her suffering, her paralysis, and private sorrows do not hinder her from influencing her son.

One feels that Mrs. Wright is a tremendous force in Richard's life, probably the most important influence on his character. She is strong in the face of overwhelming adversity. Her anger at his behavior seems far less motivated by abstract ideas of goodness than by the frustrations of her own existence. She strikes out at him because there is no one else around to strike. Those who have destroyed the possibilities of a full life for her are people she can't touch. Abandoned by her husband for another woman, she is left with herself alone, at first, and is then dependent on her family for survival. As soon as Richard is grown, she chooses to be with him, no matter how insecure the life may be.

Although Ella Wright lives by the ethics of Jim Crow, she has a dignity which cuts across those limitations. We see her always in terms of Richard, by the way he reacts to her. The reader has a feeling that she has great spirit as she endures her daily humiliations and suffering.

NATHANIEL WRIGHT

Richard's father is only very briefly presented in the book, but the effect of his personality is strong. Richard never feels close to him; he is only frightened by him. At first, in Memphis, his sleeping habits interfere with the boys' games and his temper is irrational. Later on, when Richard's mother tries to get some support from him and brings along the boy to remind him of his responsibilities, he is openly living with another woman.

The scene that takes place affects Richard not so much because of the embarrassment it causes him and his mother, but rather because his father and the strange woman seem to share a secret. His father is clearly more at ease with his new woman than he ever was with Richard's mother. They have a laughing, sensuous relationship which mocks all the suffering which Richard and his mother must endure.

Years later, when Richard meets his father again, it is in Mississippi and the old man is a sharecropper. He now represents much more than a personal memory to Richard. He represents a whole generation of black people who were driven off the land into the cities, where they were unable to cope for themselves, who were still the offsprings of slavery, and who had no more understanding of themselves historically or culturally than children. Richard is able to see his father in this clear light because he knows him so little. He can make him into a symbol of all that slavery has done to his people without having an emotional involvement interfere with his point of view. Nathaniel Wright is a victim of white tradition and white convention. His manhood can express itself in only the most elemental terms — through sexual passion, through physical labor — because any other avenue for self-expression and growth has been cut off from him. Incapable of having emotional bonds with his wife and children, he makes his roots in what is temporary, immediate satisfaction. Richard cannot hold a grudge against him for these attitudes because they are beyond his control. He is only what society has made him.

GRANNY

With her white face and black hair, her repressive religiosity and hot temper, Granny comes to represent everything that Richard must struggle to escape from. He and she are locked in warfare. It seems to be an irrational conflict at first, but soon it becomes clear that a clash of temperaments is not the only problem between them.

Hers is the first white face he knows and it is the face he dreads most. She has absorbed those qualities of white society that are intolerant, puritannical, oppressive, and fanatical. She uses the Seventh-Day Adventist faith as the weapon for all her venom, just as the white Protestants have done. She makes her church into a citadel of respectability and tyranny. Antilife, she stands in the way of Richard's natural curiosity and impulses.

The word of God is the law down to the most trivial activity. Everything that is life-giving and pleasurable — even food — is sinful, drained of its flavor in her hands. The fact that she cannot drain Richard of his energy, hopes, and boyish spirit is frightening to her. Consequently, he is doomed in the eyes of her God.

That she is physically white effectively prepares Richard for the culturally white society around him. It is ironic that what he receives from her religion — the beautiful language and the mystery of sound and meaning — is the opposite of what she wants him to receive. Austere and merciless, her character is a training ground for his development in white America.

AUTOBIOGRAPHY AND SOCIAL PROTEST

Autobiography has been, through the ages, one of the most effective forms of human protest — be it religious, political, or

personal. When one man speaks as a critic for society at large,
through the medium of his own experience, there is a validity
otherwise lacking in objective criticism. *Black Boy* has many
historical precedents — among them, St. Augustine's *Confessions*
and the *Confessions* of Jean Jacques Rousseau. However, there
are strong points of difference.

Sartre, in his essay "For Whom Does One Write," shows
what is exceptional in Richard Wright's work. He says "each
work of Wright contains what Baudelaire would have called 'a
double, simultaneous postulation' " — that is, Wright is addressing himself to two different audiences when he writes. He is
addressing both blacks and whites, and for each he needs to
supply different information. Blacks will understand readily
what he is talking about. No elaborate explanation for Wright's
experience is necessary. His purpose in addressing them, then,
is to articulate common experience and common attitudes in
order that blacks will be better equipped to deal with their own
destiny. Whites, on the other hand, cannot possibly understand
the point of view of Wright's black background. Nor can Wright
hope to have them fully see the world through his eyes. So, for
white readers, he must supply information that will have an effect entirely different from that of his own people. He must, by
his tale, induce in whites a feeling of indignation that will lead
them to act. This dual purpose, Sartre says, is what creates the
tension in Wright's work.

Wright's use of the naturalistic form is inevitable under the
circumstances. He must maintain an objective voice for his white
readers. At the same time he must write about what is most fa-
miliar — and painful — to Negroes. There is never any question
that he will tell the truth and that his words will have passion
behind them. It would not be possible to have it otherwise.

In his novels, Wright enlarged upon the themes he discovered in his own life. But fiction never has the same authority as
autobiography because art, by its very nature, is devious; an
author creates personality types and manipulates them for a
certain preconceived result. Autobiography has the revolutionary

value of "telling it like it is." At the time that he wrote *Black Boy,* Wright was immersed in Marxist ideology and Communist party activities. In an article he published in *New Challenge,* a Negro literary monthly started in 1934, he wrote:

"It is through a Marxian conception of reality and society that the maximum degree of freedom in thought and feeling can be gained for the Negro writer. Further, this dramatic Marxist vision, when consciously grasped, endows the writer with a sense of dignity which no other vision can give."

With this vision he wrote his autobiography and thereby put the reality of living experience into Marxist ideology. The book is not a mere record of personal catastrophes, but a form of social protest intended to change the society it describes.

Some of the historical events taking place around Wright, both as a boy and as a man, of course, helped to strengthen these attitudes. His father, for instance, was one among thousands of blacks involved in the Great Migration away from the southern countryside into the cities. This took place preceding and during World War I. His father was one of the casualties in this migration, so Richard was thrown back into Jim Crow society.

When Wright started his own migration northward in 1925, the country was on the brink of the Great Depression. Until the beginning of World War II, every citizen — black and white — was part of a culture suffering so badly from economic collapse that there was little opportunity to think in terms of pure art. Harlem was the center of black culture, just as Greenwich Village was a center of white culture; but both of these groups were highly influenced by political, rather than aesthetic, events.

The New Deal and communism were developing along parallel lines — each was an attempt to cope with the effects of the Depression on the country and the world. In Greenwich Village, white radicals and artists included Carl van Vechten, John Reed, Max Eastman, Walter Lippman, Lincoln Steffens, and Sinclair Lewis. In Harlem there were Langston Hughes, Claude McKay,

Countee Cullen, George S. Schuyler, Paul Robeson, Jean Toomer, and Josephine Baker. In fact, there was some contact between these groups and even a constructive exchange of ideas based on an awareness of each group's difference from the other and a search for a common ideal.

In Harlem the same ideas we hear discussed today were being discussed by the Negro intellectuals and politicians of those prewar years. Black nationalism, the Black Power movement, the matter of assimilation or integration—these were common points of difference then as now. The great exception is that communism then played a strong role in the social state of mind and many intellectuals believed that it would solve the problems of separation.

When Richard Wright was moving from Chicago to New York, therefore, the society around him was reflecting many of his own concerns. He had done some writing already for the Communist party. But *Black Boy*, even with its Marxist conclusions, was a personal record with a restricted audience. Wright was conscious of this paradox when he wrote:

"Negro writers must accept the nationalist implications of their lives, *not in order to encourage them,* but in order to change and transcend them. . . ."

By writing, then, an autobiography for a people whose political power was, to say the least, minimal, he intended to transform their minds as opposed to their lives and thereby give them the self-knowledge necessary for action. The book was bound to offend many blacks, as well as whites, for rather than glorifying anyone's image, it examined what it saw and was critical.

PERSPECTIVES ON *BLACK BOY*

Until Wright's *Native Son,* most Negro fiction was pretty much limited to historical, period pieces. Whether it belonged to the plantation tradition or the Harlem school of literature, most of it could be classed as only historically interesting. A primary reason for this is that the audience those writers addressed themselves to was middle class and "liberated" from the struggles of the poor. Since such an audience asks to read about itself, and since its spokesmen have to be "liberated" too, the writing of that time was largely restricted to a facade, a falsification of Negro life. There are, of course, notable exceptions to this rule – Jean Toomer, Zora Neale Hurston, and Langston Hughes – but as a rule, middle-class writing, black and white, was designed to entertain, not to disturb, its middle-class reader.

Therefore, when Richard leaves the South in *Black Boy*, it marks a turning point not only in his own life, but in the history of black literature. Much of the theme of his autobiography is summed up in his essay, "The Ethics of Living Jim Crow," in which he describes with awful honesty the effects of the caste system on black people. No one before Wright had written of this subject as he did and, consequently, the essay had a revolutionary value.

Wright explained how it is necessary for a people living in a society founded on free enterprise and individualism to have a background of education in one's own personal values and free access to the surrounding society. Without those qualities, and without a history of free choice, black Americans are forced to remain in close-knit, pre-individualistic groups; there, the possibility of survival is even greater than it would be if each person tried to make it on his own.

The title of *Black Boy* sums up the whole pre-individualistic ethic – or the ethics of living Jim Crow. Obviously, Wright did not think of himself as a black boy. The very term is a social judgment, not just used by white society but inherited by the black folk in Richard's life. Richard's family saw him as bad ("black"), just as the whites did, because he expressed himself as an individual. At the same time he was viewed as a boy, one who waited for and obeyed orders before he acted. The irony of this is that Richard quite clearly never did have a childhood, in the sense of a time free of responsibility or fears. His sensitivity to experience made him a man almost at birth. In the pre-individualistic, Jim Crow society he grew up in, Richard was considered evil and irrepressible.

It is important to view his autobiography in historical terms in order to understand its full significance. With the arrival of the first slaves in the seventeenth century came a culture that would be the ultimate test of the American dream. The first slaves brought with them from Africa many different ways of worshipping God and different idioms, but a common language. They also brought with them a life style which emphasized community before individualism. Under slavery these people, with their strong cultural backgrounds, were forced to absorb many of the Western customs, and they consequently evolved a culture which was completely unique — the Afro-American culture.

The devastating consequences of slavery were many, and in the two centuries preceding the Civil War, black people were integrated into society only by rape. They were disbanded, sold, and castrated by their masters. Whatever sense of community had come to these shores with them was subjected to the severest tests. One of the inevitable results was a family structure not based on blood ties, but on a larger sense of brotherhood; another result was an almost complete sense of alienation from white society. Yet another offspring of slavery was an original art form — the Blues — which incorporated African cultural forms (both linguistic and musical) with Western forms.

It wasn't until the beginning of the twentieth century that the first Blues recordings were made and that extraordinary art form was discovered by white America. The Blues had traveled underground for many years. During the Civil War, the Blues singers were like modern troubadours traveling from city to city. These poets described the effects of the war, its aftermath, the liberation of the slaves, and the work on the railroads; they described the cities and the lives within them. The songs were necessarily sad, with themes of abandonment and loneliness. The form of the Blues has since gone through many transformations, but it is always recognizable by its tone of irony and sorrow.

When Richard Wright was growing up and when he moved North, the Blues had come up from underground and set the pace of the times. Louis Armstrong, Mamie Smith, and Bessie Smith all sang of that era and its significance for the many blacks moving into the northern ghettos. Unlike their rural predecessors — Sonny Terry and Big Bill Broonzy — the new Blues singers dealt primarily with urban life.

Therefore, just as the spiritual music of the South inspired Wright, the Blues influenced the tone of his recollections. His portrait of his father is particularly relevant to that era, as is his picture of his mother, her sickness, and his grandfather's death. These are standard examples of black experiences in the beginning of this century.

And just as the Blues is expressed as a *tone* in *Black Boy*, folklore is expressed as a *style*. Every culture has its folklore which precedes and often influences the first stages of its literature. Folklore consists of stories taken from real experience, common to the group involved, and passed on by word of mouth until the story reaches the proportion of legend. Like a joke, its origins are unknown. Much of its effect is sustained by the use of dialect and references to particular group rituals. Folklore is intended to be understood only by the people in the given group, and therefore it has a cultish quality that is not conducive to reaching large audiences of people.

In *Black Boy* and certainly in a great deal of literature that came before it, folklore is a natural offspring of the social climate. Since black people were set apart from the large body of Americans, Wright expected much of his autobiography to be instantly understood by blacks, but only intellectually grasped by whites. In the incidents related to his family life in particular, this is the case. There are certain things he doesn't bother to explain because he assumes his reader will understand what he is saying. For this reason, the love between him and his mother and brother is not mentioned. Instead, he talks about only the qualities of his home life which disturb him. He takes it for granted that his black reader will know that affection exists between them. But the absence of its expression gives the book a barren and cynical tone which whites sometimes mistake for general ill will.

It must be said that this question of familial love has been a preoccupation of many other black writers. One of the many effects of slavery and pre-individualism was the repression of love between members of one family. Love was dangerous because at any time the family might be broken apart. It was dangerous because it involved an acknowledgment of individual worth. If you love your people, you are going to fight for them. "Black is beautiful" is revolutionary and dangerous to whites for just this reason. Its absence among the blacks in Wright's childhood is not surprising therefore.

The absence of love in his book will not confuse black readers. Just as the Blues is expressed as a tone of nostalgia and irony, the book's very existence is an act of love. For while it seems that Wright is interested only in escaping from his home, there is ambiguity in his flight. He is, as an artist, obsessed by his own origins. The fact that he finally left the United States for good did not mean that he was in spiritual, as well as physical, exile. As a novelist, or a fictional historian, he had to have distance in order to view his subject with some measure of sanity and proportion. Consequently he wrote of urban violence endemic to America with a clarity that shocked the nation. He didn't ask anyone to make excuses for his attitudes. They spoke for themselves, and many Americans—primarily white—were appalled by his work and were unable to face its truth.

One reviewer for the *Atlantic Monthly* reacted to *Native Son* saying: "Hatred, and the preaching of hatred, and incitement to violence can only make a tolerable relationship intolerable." As if the relationship between blacks and whites were tolerable. Indeed, it was tolerable to whites, which is an indication of the social condition that caused Wright to leave his own country.

Black writers, on the other hand, found in the legendary tale of Bigger Thomas an immediate reality. He became the figure that would dominate their work for a long time to come. In his, and Wright's, monumental stature, black writers found a truth they could address themselves to. Blacks would see themselves as the moral conscience of America after *Native Son,* although none would have such a single-minded approach to its resolution as Wright. Like Dreiser, who wrote of urban violence with a simplicity usually found in allegory only, Wright is a distinctly American product.

Naturalism, which is not the celebration of nature it sounds like, served the post-Depression writers well as a style of writing. Stark documentation of facts, the use of legal language to sum up social attitudes, and the absence of emotional values distinguished the writing of that time. For a black writer, it involved a vision of race war in America, in which all blacks are right and all whites are wrong. The simplicity of this judgment took a completely documentary form and was therefore all the more shocking.

Wright's successors — Ellison and Baldwin — would have a more complex and emotional approach to the race war. Unlike Wright, they would not view the black man's life as one of absolute despair, but would uncover joy and love as well. Only the most masochistic white reader would not be upset by Wright. It is not so evident in *Black Boy,* but in his later work, his declaration of race war is outspoken. Since he dealt with characters as historical, nearly legendary, forces, their actions are entirely ruled either by historical rage or historical guilt. In that sense they are not realistic. They act out a moral drama based on historical memory. The white people — no matter how innocent in fact they might be — are objects of justifiable revenge. The black people — no matter how immoral their individual acts might be — are historically justified; they are always right.

In *Black Boy,* the whites who enter the story are invariably mouthpieces for southern racism. They are, in a sense, as much victimized by the institution of racism as are the blacks. They do not emerge as individuals, but as contemptible types, entirely ruled by prevalent attitudes. Public opinion rules them as much as it does blacks. Richard's difficulty in assuming the role of the passive victim makes him dangerous to both communities. To identify oneself with a particular race and thereby judge one's actions according to the history of that race was never an outstanding feature of Western individualism; yet it was a well-concealed fact that whites did think of themselves in racial terms, especially when threatened by foreigners.

Wright might be criticized for being simplistic in his judgments, but the reader must confront at all times the conditions that produced such a writer—a writer so thoroughly American—and in the light of those conditions accept and reckon with his presence. *Black Boy* explains what those conditions were and, in doing so, introduces Richard Wright to America as a human fact.

REVIEW QUESTIONS

1. What are the advantages (both personal and political) of autobiography as a literary form?

2. What are the implications of the title of *Black Boy?*

3. What does Richard's father come to represent in Richard's life?

4. How does a pre-individualistic society reveal itself in Granny's household?

5. Discuss the question of love, and its lack, in *Black Boy.*

6. Describe the significance for Richard of Uncle Thomas, Griggs, and Shorty.

7. In what ways are folklore and the Blues relevant to *Black Boy?*

8. How does Richard treat white people as opposed to blacks? Is there a different judgment between his attitudes to each group?

9. What is the similarity in Richard's reactions to Miss Simon and Mrs. Moss? Explain why he reacts this way to them.

10. How are Granny and Addie responsible for Richard's attitudes? How do they contribute to his becoming a rebel and an artist?

11. In what ways is Richard Wright typical of American writers?

12. How does *Black Boy* express an ideology in the incidents described? What is that ideology?

13. What is the social significance of the fight between Richard and Harrison? What does the fight teach Richard about racism?

14. How does Richard look upon himself? At what points does he disapprove of his own actions, and why?

15. Why was *Black Boy* a landmark in Afro-American literature?

SELECTED BIBLIOGRAPHY

ALGREN, N. "Remembering Richard Wright." *Nation* (January, 1961), 85-87.

BALDWIN, JAMES. "The Survival of Richard Wright." *Nation* (March, 1961), 52-53.

BASSO, HAMILTON. "Thomas Jefferson and the Black Boy." *New Yorker*, XXI (March 10, 1945), 86.

BONE, ROBERT A. *The Negro Novel in America.* New Haven: Yale University Press, 1958.

BROWN, STERLING A. "Criticism of Richard Wright." *Nation* (*April, 1938*), 448.

BURGAN, EDWARD B. *The Art of Richard Wright's Short Stories.* New York: Oxford University Press. 1947.

CAIN, ALFRED E., *et al. The Negro Heritage Library.* New York: Educational Heritage Incorporated, 1968.

COHN, DAVID L. "The Negro Novel: Richard Wright." *Atlantic Monthly*, CLXV (May, 1940), 659-61.

ELLISON, RALPH. "Richard Wright's Blues." *Antioch Review Anthology*, ed., PAUL BIXLER. New York: World Publishing Co., 1953.

ESTES, RICE. "Freedom to Read." *Library Journal*, LIV (December 15, 1960), 4421-22.

HARRINGTON, OLLIE. "The Last Days of Richard Wright." *Ebony*, LXXVII (February, 1969), 83-86.

HICKS, GRANVILLE. "The Power of Richard Wright." *Saturday Review*, XX (October 18, 1958), 65.

HOWE, IRVING. "Richard Wright: A Word of Farewell." *New Republic* (February, 1961), 17-18.

CARL MILTON HUGHES. *The Negro Novelist (1940-50).* New York: Citadel Press, 1953.

JONES, H. M. "Up from Slavery: Richard Wright's Story." *Saturday Review of Literature*, XXVIII (March 3, 1945), 9.

JONES, LEROI. *Blues People.* London: MacGibbon and Kee, 1965.

KENNEDY, RAYMOND. "A Dramatic Autobiography," *Yale Review*, XXXIV (Summer, 1945), 762.

KUNTZ, R. *Twentieth Century Authors*. New York: H. W. Wilson Co., 1955.

MARGOLIES, EDWARD. *The Art of Richard Wright*. Carbondale: Southern Illinois University Press, 1969.

MCCALL, DAN. *The Example of Richard Wright*. New York: Harcourt, Brace and World, Inc., 1969.

PRESCOTT, ORVILLE. *In My Opinion*. New York: Bobbs-Merrill Company, Inc., 1932.

PLOSKI, HARRY A., and ROSCOE BROWN. "Richard Wright." *The Negro Almanac II* (1968), 49-50.

RUSSELL, TONY. *Blacks, Whites and Blues*. New York: Stein and Day, 1970.

WEBB, CONSTANCE. *Richard Wright: A Biography*. New York: G. P. Putnam's Sons, 1968.

WHITE, RALPH K. "*Black Boy:* A Value Analysis." *Journal of Abnormal Psychology*, XLIII (October, 1947), 44.

NOTES

Your Guides to Successful Test Preparation.

Cliffs Test Preparation Guides
• Complete • Concise • Functional • In-depth

Efficient preparation means better test scores. Go with the experts and use *Cliffs Test Preparation Guides*. They focus on helping you know what to expect from each test, and their test-taking techniques have been proven in classroom programs nationwide. Recommended for individual use or as a part of a formal test preparation program.

Publisher's ISBN Prefix 0-8220

Qty.	ISBN	Title	Price	Qty.	ISBN	Title	Price
	2078-5	ACT	8.95		2044-0	Police Sergeant Exam	9.95
	2069-6	CBEST	8.95		2047-5	Police Officer Exam	14.95
	2056-4	CLAST	9.95		2049-1	Police Management Exam	17.95
	2071-8	ELM Review	8.95		2076-9	Praxis I: PPST	9.95
	2077-7	GED	11.95		2017-3	Praxis II: NTE Core Battery	14.95
	2061-0	GMAT	9.95		2074-2	SAT*	9.95
	2073-4	GRE	9.95		2325-3	SAT II*	14.95
	2066-1	LSAT	9.95		2072-6	TASP	8.95
	2046-7	MAT	12.95		2079-3	TOEFL w/cassettes	29.95
	2033-5	Math Review	8.95		2080-7	TOEFL Adv. Prac. (w/cass.)	24.95
	2048-3	MSAT	24.95		2034-3	Verbal Review	7.95
	2020-3	Memory Power for Exams	5.95		2043-2	Writing Proficiency Exam	8.95

Prices subject to change without notice.

Available at your booksellers, or send this form with your check or money order to **Cliffs Notes, Inc.,** P.O. Box 80728, Lincoln, NE 68501 http://www.cliffs.com

☐ Money order   ☐ Check payable to Cliffs Notes, Inc.

☐ Visa ☐ Mastercard   Signature_____

Card no. _____ Exp. date _____

Signature _____

Name _____

Address _____

City _____ State_____ Zip_____

*GRE, MSAT, Praxis PPST, NTE, TOEFL and Adv. Practice are registered trademarks of ETS. SAT is a registered trademark of CEEB.

T ... Again

Now ...
Revie...
more introductory level courses. Use Quick Reviews to increase your understanding of fundamental principles in a given subject, as well as to prepare for quizzes, midterms and finals.

Think quick with new Cliffs Quick Review titles. You'll find them at your bookstore or by returning the attached order form. Do better in the classroom, and on papers and...

...eviews.

CLIFFS QUICK REVIEW GEOMETRY

Publisher's ISBN Prefix 0-8220

Qty.	ISBN	Title	Price	Total	Qty.	ISBN	Title	Price	Total
	5302-0	Algebra I	7.95			5324-1	Economics	7.95	
	5303-9	Algebra II	9.95			5329-2	Geometry	9.95	
	5300-4	American Government	9.95			5330-6	Human Nutrition	9.95	
	5301-2	Anatomy & Physiology	9.95			5331-4	Linear Algebra	9.95	
	5304-7	Basic Math & Pre-Algebra	9.95			5333-0	Microbiology	9.95	
	5306-3	Biology	7.95			5337-3	Physics	7.95	
	5312-8	Calculus	7.95			5349-7	Statistics	7.95	
	5318-7	Chemistry	7.95			5358-6	Trigonometry	7.95	
	5320-9	Differential Equations	9.95			5367-5	Writing Grammar, Usage, & Style	9.95	

Prices subject to change without notice.

Available at your booksellers, or send this form with your check or money order to **Cliffs Notes, Inc., P.O. Box 80728, Lincoln, NE 68501** http://www.cliffs.com

get the Cliffs Edge!

☐ Money order ☐ Check payable to Cliffs Notes, Inc.

☐ Visa ☐ Mastercard   Signature_____

Card no. _____ Exp. date_____

Name _____

Address _____

City _____ State_____ Zip_____

DEC 0 6 2011